T0244776

RISK

RISK

Rusty Morrison

Black Ocean
Boston · Chicago

Black Ocean
P.O. Box 52030
Boston, MA 02205
blackocean.org

ISBN: 978-1-939568-76-2

Library of Congress Control Number: 2024930656

Printed in Canada

FIRST EDITION

TABLE OF CONTENTS

THAT WOMAN YESTERDAY

That woman yesterday had   no margin between her one
face crossing San Pablo Ave   and the face already in
a new epoch, the car she   never saw strike her. Each face

in motion within you. Here   in what you are about to
type. Within the movement of   words closer to consequence.
Even as realities   collapse between this word and

what you thought would be the next.   Just as realities will.
Or so says the eleventh   century apocalypse
prophet Joachim. Let these words   fragment what they intend to

count. You saw willow leaves fall   to where you know they will leak
out of their skins. On the small   patch of ground surrounded by
concrete where you saw a few   land. Where time will cause in them

an elsewhere effect. Their next   epoch is being soil. Will
any of the selves you are   migrate as they do? No words
will tell you which self. Or what   epoch it might travel to.

LINING THE SIDEWALK WHERE YOU WALK

Lining the sidewalk where you   walk the block each night at dusk
are trees. Can't name their species,   let alone where their image
in your mind has taken root.   Tonight they each seem to let
fall a shadow in your path,   more than the sun's setting could
cause. What is "cause"? How would you   really know to what or whom
it belongs? Do you even   know what causes might compel
you and from what conditions   they might arise? This tree seems
inscrutable, foliaged   in its anonymity.
Do you know as little of   your neighbors? Is this even
how you live day to day with   Ken, your husband? You do know
his given name but what name   does he wear within himself?
Does it change annually   or is he perennial?
Walk around the block again,   you're not ready to go home.
Are these the same trees they were   45 minutes ago?
Open your front door, does your   key fit the lock? Have you
already converted this   stranger into whoever
you just believe him to be?   Outside is the gloaming hour.
Ask this man you call Ken to   go back into it with you,
to listen for the private,   plosive anarchies that might
be wind in the branches, or   the exhaling of earth that's
covered in concrete. Here, too,   a loud chorus of sighs from
the neighbors' open windows.   Sounds you've never tried to hear
or comprehend, but could you?   Is it better to try, fail?

But recognize how something   inexplicable comes, as
a sensitivity that's   beyond price? You recall Ken's
sighing, what you hear each night,   but ignore, as if a sigh
could ever be meaningless,   be it husband's, be it wind's,
be it leaves falling right here   that you'll never see again.

YOU ARE OUTSIDE ALONE, NEAR THE END OF YOUR WALK

You are outside alone, near   the end of your walk, but you
don't want to go home. A wind   has risen with the sunset.
Feel in it sounds you've not heard   as wind, weren't they always there?
Has something that you keep shut   opened by a crack? A mind
delves into any lack of   clarity—moon suddenly
gone green in the movie you   were watching, then shifting back
to white. In the film no one   mentions it, making it more
sensation than visual   as a significator.
You watch for it when standing   in front of your house after
dusk and waiting for moonrise.   You've read this somewhere—"what is
inexplicable   lodges more deeply than what's
easily known." You stand now   in this bracing wind, sensing
small hollows in air currents,   which expose, then obscure, sounds.
Will these sounds amass into   meanings you will remember,
write down, keep some part of their   mystery alive in you
and feel that mystery grow?   You ask yourself, asking in
the voice of the child who would   listen inside herself, not
to her mother's voice. A child   you were, and you mostly try
to forget. That child shut out   the sky your mom was to you,
the rushing wind of her voice.   Wind can cause such damage. Last autumn,
power lines fell, cut power   for some days. The lack killed your
elderly neighbor. She   didn't ask for help when her
medicine spoiled in her fridge.   Minds can't stop delving into
any lack of clarity;   they can't stop looking. What will

you harrow from confusion   as you take this walk in wind,
then stand still and listen? What   might you cultivate?
after all the difficult   harrowing—drawing yourself
over the hard rocky ground,   that is your own. Trusting there'll
be a path for seeds to be   planted and grow. In last night's
movie, you saw farmers who   were ruined by the dust bowl.
Not a single plant would grow,   all the top soil blown away
before they knew what they'd lost.   Farmers you are afraid you've
become. A movie with a   last scene that looks, for just one
moment—the director's trick—   as if there were, everywhere
trees. But the ground hasn't healed.   Tonight you see your own trick
of a director's eye—here   are pantomimes in each of
the most subtle gestures of   leaves. Inexplicable, at
least for now, as the dark   envelopes them. They, and you
with them, seem to disappear.   You are surprised but it comes
easefully, until all that   remains is the sensation
of inexplicable change.

BLEACH TREES

Bleach trees down to one tree. Down   to one inward curling leaf
that you want to watch turn in   wind it floated through and fall
transparent into words on   this page. But no memory

is an actual leaf bleached   of all but your desire
to see it again and now   to feel it fall through you. More
solid than you are. Write your   page-a-day in tight constraints

as if ideas that perch deep   in language's branches might
be teased into anything   more than a nostalgia you
conjure for a kind of work   that you have spent years wanting

to achieve. Where a chirrup   and stem is pronounced but no
bird need be exhaustively   described between them for it
to sing. Give it up. Just write   into abandonment. Carve

away what you volunteer   as portraiture. A pair of
spectacles with bright orange   construction paper glued on
for eyes. Realize how this   injures what you needn't understand

even as in your words it   comes to you and is seeking
an anonymity in   granulated sugar poured
slow from a bucket onto
snow.

IT'S HERE AT YOUR FAMILIAR STREET-CORNER

It's here at your familiar   street-corner in the morning's
rushed traffic, you realize   a woman is in you. She

has maybe always been here   staring, through your eyes, outward
at others. Her eyes are bees   foraging out from a hive

they've spent years making without   their letting you taste more than
bee-sting. You've grown the busy   colony of her, within

the wild occluded landscape   unnervingly most present
in your dreams. Or has it been   she, who has cultivated

you as an outward cell that   protects the grub-like larvae
within? Or do you use now   the otherness of bees to

ignore what you will only   let yourself see as the life
of grubs still-born within you,   the life you've never become?

A STRANGER BEFORE YOU IS WAITING

A stranger before you is   waiting on the streetme corner.
She is a field of gold wheat   that might have made many fine
loaves of bread, had the field not   burned in a conflagration
that spits at you through her eyes.   You recognize in her eyes
what she recognizes in   your own, that an unfinished
plot is being dug for her   in the scorched earth. A space made
for this woman, of 5'4", same   height as you. The digging has
gone on a long time. You see   it is her own hands doing
what they've been, for all her life,   taught to do. Dirt on her face,
same grime in your mirror.   Material survives long
past whatever meaning is   subscribed to it. Two streets meet,
two women face each other.   Meaning dissipates. They are
just the material of   the clashing sound of chords in
a piano where a cat   has landed. All four feet find
footing, make for an instant   a world shifting all meaning
in which you believe. Shock is   substance made of suddenness
that can halt every car, bus,   speeding past, can sometimes shake
the few trees, even as thick   trunked as they are, planted years
past in this sidewalk. A black   upright piano. The cat
curls into a nest of sleep   on its keys. You recognize
you've made meaning of it, as   the piano your Nonna
kept polished by her window.   Never were you to touch it
with your dirty hands. The sound   of its chords now is hollow,
an echo of a life that you   never made into meanings
you could live. The woman is   staring at you, she nods, she
never lived her life either.   Her memories are her own

hollow core. A hollowness   is dangerous, you know this.
You've let yourself be filled with   the promise of a civil
life by men who would ransack   even emptiness, steal that
from you. You reach down, your hands   pick up dirt, good rich topsoil.
Dirt more alive than you'd thought   dirt could be—small spiraling
worms you see might call down birds,   wild and rich in their winged life.
You might grow life in that dirt.   She reaches down, too, even
though you both stand on sidewalk   where no rich black soil should be.

NARROW NEGOTIATIONS (1st)

When the clock ticks out caged mice
not minutes. You hide in bed.

Still you hear their treadmill spin.
Hear it in the sound of your

cereal poured in a bowl.
No wonder you have trouble

swallowing. As you chew aren't
the mice weary. Spent. Aren't you?

Their teeth are sharp. They'll soon
rip free of the containment

of this page. Just behind it
your past's beliefs spy on you

exhausted by all the ways
you move their meanings around.

YOU RUB

You rub the just-picked poppy   petal between thumb and
first finger until orange   is your prisoner. Just like
squeezing yourself between one   politic act and the next.

Leaving just trace color. Hard   even to recognize as
an adaptation you once   thought would breed safety.
A compressed petal isn't   pretty. Is pressure really

your ally? Does exerting   force always put you in charge?
You have sex under tight sheets   just to feel how skin is such
a thin containment for what's   dispossessed inside you as

the sheets too easily give   way. Orphaned in air sometimes
you close your eyes spit over   the side of the world any
world. Open them and see there's   dampness on your husband's face.

Residue of hot tears he   won't wipe away. The air thick
with steam. It's a mirror of   what bodies are: just heat and
surrender. You're excess but   don't know it. Will you feel when

you turn into pure static
sweetly pungent as heated
tar?

YOU ENVY CYCLISTS' CAREEN THROUGH GRIDLOCK

You envy cyclists' careen   through gridlock. Chrome-spokes flash. They
defy damage. You're afraid   this enthrall is disloyal

to the halo you'd have to   X out in the self-portrait
of safety that's taken years   to complete. Destroy it in

an instant? Begin again?   This one would be entitled "Risk."
What Stein calls masterpiece can't   be planned then staged with the
small

figurines you keep in your   sleeve. They've memorized what you
expect them to perform. What   you are doing is praying

to gods who will adjust like   suspenders. Shred their clothes and
find them transparent. Find just   background where you're left alone.

That's when cyclists dismount. They've   brought fresh apples still cold but
will you dare to ask for one?

YOU REMEMBER YESTERDAY

You remember yesterday.   A cop who stopped you speeding.
His face with no rest in it   behind his performance of

force, the pull of his anger   is tidal. Had he stopped you
two hours later into   his shift, then nothing could have

protected you from drowning   in his rising waters.
He has made you get out of   your car. Why does the shadow

of a gull, as it crosses   this imagined beach where you
feel yourself stand before him,   make you drop your scarf in waves

rushing toward you? Don't step back.   This wave won't drown you. This time.
The wave has your scarf. You could   wade in for it. Then would you

risk submersing yourself in   his belief about you? Just
another fool-woman who   will be someone's victim, who

needs to be taught a lesson.   How easily from her skin
wounds will grow, thick weeds she'll be   lost in. He could show her how

devastated a garden   she'll soon become. He sees you
standing against the tide, still   upright against all he is.

But you are lucky today.   Your imagined scarf is still
visible to you, something   you can retrieve, hold onto.

Still damp, still yours, much as this   sense you discern from watching
his eyes—you aren't worth so much   paperwork he'd need to file.

THE GROCERY STORE OWNER

The grocery store owner   is at his register once
again this morning facing   you with his outline as you
face him with yours. Between you   the conversation admits
to nothing that's inside your   outline nor his—yet there is
a wheelbarrow he brought from   Yemen, full of empty sacks.
He left his country before   he had to use them as bags
for bodies of relatives   whom he believes are now dead.
You purchase real milk yogurt   that you know you'll have to will
yourself to eat today. You   know that your life depends on
the power of your will to   choose to eat and feel full, to
choose eating over the will   to control your hunger—a
control you've believed in when   all else in your life is so
precarious. There's danger   everywhere. The worst dangers
are those you can't predict. This   man behind the register
knows this. He has eyes that need   not change in expression for
you to see that the sacks he   carries will grow heavier
the longer you look at him.   He lets you keep looking at
him. He does not look away.

TRAGEDY HAS NO TRACTION

Tragedy has no traction   when you're eating cereal.
It's three a.m. Count each lost   soul afloat face-down in your
cold failure rate. Your faith in   personal change just won't hold

water. Ask anyone who's   pulling at the oars in their
leaky-boat concept with all   their might. Already shedding
emergency equipment   disclosures from certified

visionaries. You've largely   ceased to translate old theories
you depended on into   meanings already past their
sell-date before you finish.

HEAR NEWS ANCHORS

Hear news anchors, then bank clerks,   adopt a new accent. This
next popular speech tactic   arrives inarguable.
Now it's personally yours.   "Power penetrates bodies,"
says Foucault, "to govern from   inside." Mostly soundlessly.

But you'll soon hear us all used   as history's peculiar
alliance, built simply of   its passage. Plus some friction
caused by the indefinite   articles that any new
deception drags with it. Did   you think words would help you to

self-police and syllables   could be tamed by counting them?
Thought you'd tempt what Keats saw *light-   winged in some melodious
plot* to befriend you in your   failure to be anything
more than a fugitive in   the *shadows numberless*. Are

there subversive songbirds who   still harmonically do
transmit *thou wast not born for   death*, but now, along the new
fiber optics? Could words come   that would kin you to others
who suffer equally what   you sense remains answerless?

Can you write what isn't known   to you? Will lyric hear it?

LOOK TO YOUR RIGHT

Look to your right, as you drive   the freeway this morning. Roll
down all your windows. The wind   isn't sentient, at least

that you'll understand as a   sentience. Still, the wind does
feel alive to you, awake to   its release of air. From it

comes a release of your own,   pent up tics and frayed nerves. How
many hours, even days,   have you been holding your breath?

Avoiding breathing? Hasn't   it been a defiance of
living you've not let yourself   see as an insolence that

harms only you? Even if   it somehow seemed to become
a mastery, a skill? Here   now, driving to work, parking

the car. Breathe out the child who   you no longer must be now,
that child you were—so frightened,   alone. Your mother, always

driving the highways, but not   heading to anywhere. You,
in the passenger seat, eyes   turned away from her as much

as she'd allow that freedom   to an elsewhere adulthood
would someday offer to you.   How sure you were then that, if

you were behind the wheel, you'd   know exactly where to go.
Places a road could take you.

NARROW NEGOTIATIONS (2nd)

Wet clothes on the line revolve.
A door you can't pass. See shapes

of bodies you thought you were
in damp cotton-jeans silk-shirts.

Feel the person that tight-sized
clothing tells you to believe.

But she's not there. Just behind
the glass. Even if fingers

aren't scar tissue. Still you press
hard past sensation. The air

hurricanes but the door won't
open an inch. Though the shape

seems to revolve. No feeling
you trust offers you access.

THROUGH YOUR OPEN WINDOW

Through your open window come   radio beams from unmarked
trucks indoctrinating all   susceptible fools, not just
you, to buy easy rub-off   dignity. It's not what you

bargained for when you sewed up   your sackcloth into a doll
of politics, easy to   endorse, stuffed it with a smile
that coughs a little more each   time you can afford it less.

Your glands weep contaminants.   Try the new lemon-scent sold
to all of us with lungs who   mortgage away our air. Choke
in spit from chewing on a   gloss ad's luxury skyline

where you too can lack nothing
enjoy the billion dollar
view.

NO WILD POPPIES

No wild poppies in your weeds.   Exhaust yourself waiting and
watching. A kind of watching   that's like lying down in what
should be a margin between   you and death. Believe death is
a long way on the far side   of growing things. You need to
watch the soil. How volunteer   seedlings of foxgloves only
grow where other plants have died.   Every plant needs death to eat
or it will starve. Starving is   the only option some have.
You try the latest hair gel,   in order to stiffen up
against worse damage you might   do to yourself. But stiff hair
will seed in itself harm that   advertisements won't admit.
Denying how easily   brittle fears will break you, if
you let them. You spend every   spare hour watching from your
window, not letting yourself   know what you're waiting for. Then
you glimpse an orange color,   on one wild poppy, then more.
All are holding the echo   of sunrise chiming a pale
luminescence, even hours   into the afternoon's heat.
A mind can wait for decades   for color it'd never
let itself recognize to   bloom within it. You watched as
your friend lived wildly into   her death in ways she'd never
lived in her whole lifetime. Will   you let yourself wait so long?

REFRIGERATOR'S HUM

What are you living for? Asks   the refrigerator's hum.
Serene as you imagine   death to be. What is it you
are hungry for? The pleasure   you feel when what you tell your
husband scares him. This starving   and how you think you hide it.
His interference with your   calm aggravates. You nearly
show it. Pretend to listen.   Listening is building
a hum that the frig teaches.   Inside it's all ice and what
you know is preserving you.   Your fingers fidget a strand
of your hair. You realize   gestures can't be trusted. This
one making conspicuous   misery that you deny.
It's morning again. So soon.   Here is the next open page
of your getting-up-again   story. These days will just bloom
for your dried-stick willfulness.   Call it "reality" but
writing such denial makes   words in your journal wreckage
receptacles. You want to   trust that starving yourself seals
what's inside you. As safe as   any fridge's door. Meaning
seepage is containable.   The containment guaranteed.
You have had a natural   wariness toward any such
promises. At least shouldn't   you diagnose that loss of
suspicion as due to fear?

IT'S LATE

It's late. Find a movie you   recognize. You won't watch as
much as remember. Choose   to believe memory is
a wool blanket for the chill   that your own thinness causes.
Recite the familiar lines   along with them. No matter
how well, you're still shivering.   Tonight, even though it's dark,
turn off the TV, go back   out to walk in the weed patch
that once was your yard. Rather   than watching for poppies you
look up and see there are stars.   Not just the brighter ones you've
glanced at many times before.   A grey-tinged point in the sky
hardly visible beyond   the usual stars turns soft
to your imaginings. Turns   blue as if you were moving
nearer and seeing blue is   its color. Seeing how it
is steadfast. The way you once   heard high notes that Coltrane reached
and then held as no one could.   As though one high note could fill
with the breath of everyone   listening. His note living in
every lung. Expanding as   is this blue point within you.

IT'S FIRST DAYLIGHT AND THE WRECKED POSSIBLE

It's first daylight and the wrecked   possible is not yet a
foregone conclusion. But you   already hear what's digging
for you with its long fetching   pole. Just like everybody

else you squeeze down a little   deeper inside your muddy
syntax hiding some meaning   here and there in soft dirt
while what's burrowing moves close.   You toss the luxury of

moral consequence out with   collective catastrophe
like so much ground-up gravel.   Already the morning's gone
humid and asthmatic but   its little cough could be a

friendly reminder of what
comes when you mix ink and smoke.

HERE IN YOUR BACKYARD

Here in your backyard lie down.   You've come to resist the pull
of the choice to starve using   your will or eat using your
will. As if there were any   difference. You close your eyes
against night sky and feel how   you want it. Feel what it means
to give in to whatever   you'll find. Cloudy night. No stars.
The oldest wound opening   is fertile ground where you must
take care of what otherwise   will fill with the old damage.
Let it breathe here in your yard.   Two breaths between closing and
opening your eyes. You pause.   You can choose to pause. Before
whatever the next instant   will ask. Before whatever
you'll receive from what's only   the memory of a soft
blue point deep in sky's distance.   A point you allow isn't
here and you can't control might   appear or not from behind
this fog. No, you're not ready   to let imagination
be enough. To feel that. Is   this a hunger you can stand
waiting for? What you knew was   waiting in the images
of William Blake. How he found   his way to illuminate
that *nature has no outline*   *but imagination has*
super-fluid contours that   flood the narrow container
that will is making of you.

NARROW NEGOTIATIONS (3rd)

First bite of apple-slice makes
savor sing. Clairvoyant. Past

and future warbling as you
chew. The next bite is only

silenced preservation. Stuffed
songbird. Third bite will just taste

of the taxidermist's pride
in skillful resemblances.

How surprisingly sour what's
left. Necessary to dull

sensation. An ornate cage
must be built for what remains

to rationalize why your
ardencies go fugitive.

CROWDED MONDAY BART TRAIN

Crowded Monday BART train. Its   mindlessness botanical.
You take the first seat. Claim it   for your age. Your shirt smelling
already like somebody   else's sweat. A toddler is
crashing against your leg. His   mom gives him a sucker he
hasn't figured out how to   fit inside his mouth. You taste
the instant's sumptuous pause   between flavors to relish,
then confusion and choking   on what was trusted would bring
only pleasure and not faith   lost. An erosion begun.
You trust short-term incentives.   Isn't it really the same?
Why do you avoid asking   the cost? You leave the BART car.
One-way gates right in front of   you spit you out. Imagine
your genes passing through their gates   into the pool where your self
as you know her will be lost.

HAND-OUT DOLLAR

Hand-out dollar ready in   your pocket. Subway rush-hour
a thick o'clock of bodies.   Stoop-shouldered shabby old men
all wear your dad's unshaved face.

You carry his sack of soiled   civility. A fool's pride.
Just look how precisely all   eye your thin-scabbed privacy.
Too easily it leaks your

paltry cash. Your earth-friendly   button's blue defenselessness
would be more beautiful on   a new plasma screen. It'll look
just like seawater. No one

swims in their own contracting   metaphor for long before
it grays. What you highlighted   blonde. Thought you could change colors.
Thought you were renewing nouns.

SOME DAYS EVERYONE IS WELL CONCEALED

Some days everyone is well   concealed by their assumptions.
Then maybe an ambulance   siren. Too close. It squeezes
all of you together. As   fear siphons off a little
more anonymity. So   you turn in unison glad
for the others near you. Feel   a communal breath taken
and released. The siren is   a dormant virus again.
When you turn the corner. Walk   a block. Here are five people
in line at the ATM   so separately together—
requires a vigilance   easy to mistake for calm.

DEEP FOG ON THE STREET

Deep fog on the street coming   visible under street lights.
If you walk out the door you'll   be lost. A sense of being
the lost thing grows dimensions   that are more evocative
the longer you allow it.   Opening you to other
sensations your body's cells   emit. A condensation
of emotions suffuses   your senses and inspires your
hand to risk. To reach and find   the door's knob in your grip. For
your legs to bring you across.   Consider the word "threshold"
and imagine yourself as   a person in early dawn
a century ago. You   have strong arms threshing wheat. Walk
out the door into the skill   that is a field of workers.
Outside are droplets of rain   moving in unison which
you feel more than see. Some forms   of attention won't come from
what's before you. Won't come from   memory that you have lived.
You needn't have words for what   arrives from all the selves and
more than the selves that you are.   Clouds break open so very
far above that it is part   intuition to see how
rain is just now beginning.   Say "you" in this life. She'll be
anyone. Look inside what   you might mean by "a moment"
that is "this moment" and see it as   no elsewhere but this and this
and this as the changing shape   you can enter at any
place you stand. Here's a shape that   opens into the cycle
of harvests that is every   alternative artist you
are.

NARROW NEGOTIATIONS (4th)

Pine needles dead on the limb
blur as wind shivers them loose

from their outlines for a split
instant then each snaps back. Wind

is a workshop of freedoms
that only intuition

turned kaleidoscopic can
perceive. What is it you've been

dead to that's within yourself?
Your outline is breathing. Look.

See a world of new lives form
the death in you fertilized

to let each instant you live
riot with new frequencies.

IT'S PAST DUSK TONIGHT

It's past dusk tonight. You walk   out of the house away from
the question What will you do   now? You've faced locked abstinence.
Bone-door you've carved to wear your   mother's face. Tonight's full moon
alters shadows as if she   moves bone with no flesh left to
mask how her face starved before   her body. Premonition
needn't be prophecy. Will   you chew the glazed donut down
to its soft inexistence?   A sensation you crave. Then
spit out what's in your mouth? All   of it? Keeping the bone door
locked. You've read in your dog-eared   Cioran that a mystic's
way is abstinence. What you've   found convenient to believe.

THE ONLY EVIDENCE

The only evidence you   exist is this impulse to
starve, to know willpower comes   the way a full moon rises.
In the sky, there is only   moon's outline. You've hidden it,
full, wide, and white in your mouth.   Your mother's face was as white
in death. Too many nights show   in your mirror's reflection
how she rises unbidden.   Starving can sharpen vision.
Look through her face to the dark   of the moon's echo-features.
What evidence is there, in   you, is also an echo,
insubstantial as any   memory, however it
began, however sourced   from material substance.
Can you slip inside echo, and claim its source as your own?
Claim as your own whatever   you find there? Outside you hear
the mockingbird nested in   its obscurity. There it
can enact other birds' songs.   Insistent out your window.
Its instinct cultivates space   within itself to store more
stolen song, more evidence   of what its existence is
becoming. How to make your   hollow inside yourself as
wide? You have been hungry for   an emptiness in you to
control. The real moon grows full   then waxes then disappears.
Today you'll give a dollar   to a woman. Three times you've
seen her standing half a block   from the post office's door,
sometimes she is much closer.   Did a postal clerk warn her
how far away from the door   she must stay? Do you think to
starve makes you invisible   to the threats that come to you?
Your hand is holding a piece   of toasted bread. One more than
you'd planned to eat. Is that will   to eat it so much different

than the will to starve? How can   you find evidence of your
existence in either? You   are in the car in front of
the post office waiting for   what might arise between you and
the woman with her small jar   for money—some sensation
more uncertain than will. To   feel, even fleetingly, as
evidence that you exist.

AN UNFILTERED CIGARETTE IN THE YOUNG WOMAN'S GREEN LIPS

An unfiltered cigarette   in the young woman's green lips.
In her eyes a long-legged   stare across museum steps.
Draw your eyes up to her eyes'   height. Glimpse what may be future
moving—darting rodents that will come   at night, quick-witted, sharp teethed.
She draws on her cigarette,   calm-eyed. You feel yourself choke
on your own attempt to sigh   casually. It's as if her
silent laughter could be caught   in your lungs. You cough, you are
no longer young, you know it.   You'll never again feel safe.
The future is watching you;   the young woman watches it.
You lived inside green lips once,   you ignored older women,
never noticing their eyes,   what they were always hiding.

INSIDE THE MUSEUM, FIND

Inside the museum, find   framed paintings—most are gilt-trimmed,
well-polished aggrandizements   that dull eyes, slow vision's skill,
obscuring how the masters'   paintings hold hidden ghosts, gods.
What is a masterwork? But   the result of the "endlessness"
that demands an artist seek   to reach unrelentingly
beyond death, toward whatever   that artist must risk, to make
palpable, the human stakes   most of us won't dare witness
consciously. An artist must   choke, if need be, to inhale
the thinnest air of human   trials, failings—whatever will
flow from his, her, their blood to   hands, willing hands to defy
any convention, defy   any socially sanctioned
conviction of what "art" is   allowed to show and who is
allowed to make "art." All this,   the artist of any time
must hazard with each brushstroke.   What is within the colors,
the composition of forms,   contrast between the foreground,
background, of art? What god or   ghost presence draws both artist
and art-viewer alike toward   perceptions of otherwise
lost or denied pasts, glimpses   of futures they will avoid
imagining—all of their   parched deserts, drowned children,
blackened skies, so seemingly   forgivable omissions,
their lies of convenience, all   their willfully accepted
oblivions now exposed.

HER GLANCE CAUGHT YOU AS YOU SCALE THE MUSEUM STEPS

Her glance caught you as you scale   the museum steps. She sees
you staring at her Dunhill,   as yet unlit, sees your face
retreat from envy, sees how   you savor a memory
then you retreat from that, too.   Her eyes laugh, in the way that
only the young's eyes can laugh,   both unguarded and performed.
Though it seems she has entered   this room of artworks ahead,
she is nowhere to be seen.   Where could she have gone? Into
an artwork. Something is lit   behind the painted woman's
eyes in this one, eyes portrayed   by a woman artist who
found in them room for viewers   with the courage to step in,
light a cigarette, look round.   The young woman with green lips
has just inhaled, drawn deeply   on her Dunhill, filling her
lungs with a future that seems   will last, as if future won't
come to be burned down to ash.

PROP UP AN IRONING BOARD

Prop up an ironing board.   Let its featureless face be
your mirror. Rub its silence   on your cheeks as rouge until
they disappear. Now you'll brave   tearing strips of skin from your
tongue to set loose in wind. *What's   meant is never found* rejoins
Benjamin. He knew the glass   stairs that crack as you descend.
"Shatter" is your frequency.   Find there the *zone surrounding*
the intoxication wrote   Benjamin where *ground is silk.*

NARROW NEGOTIATIONS (5th)

Chaff of today's news cycle.
But you'd meant to type "chafe" not

"chaff." Walk in this sudden field.
You have work to do. Winnow

away the thick husk of your
expected direction. Find

her eyes. A woman last month
who sat down in the BART seat

across from you. Her bloodshot
eyes were chaos. Your chaos

is bloodshot too. Memory
is a fertile field of your

archived emergencies. Watch
her watch no one, which is you.

YOUR REAL MEANINGS CAN'T SURVIVE, THEY REMAIN TRANSLUCENT FISH

Your real meanings can't survive,   they remain translucent fish
you chew and swallow before   they escape your mouth, meanings
with mangled fins. Only bones   do you spit at your husband.
He makes runes, casts them each day.   His divination tells you
"denial," "defiance," "false   obedience." None live in
your mouth long enough to spawn.   He never lies about words
to you, never says he sees   "forgiveness." You cut your hair
staring at your haphazard   wielding of sharp scissors. He
tells you it's layered, to him,   it's not only violence.
You want to see through his eyes,   not the dead-fish eyes you wear.

TIDAL WAVES FLOOD OUT

Tidal waves flood from your mouth   instead of words. Wave after
wave. Your husband sees he must   swim through them. He tells you
he's
patient, that he can hold air   in his lungs for a long time.
He says it's inherited.   His mother won long-distance
swimming championships. She   disappeared in the tide for
what seemed much too long, then she   appeared at the finish line.
Tidal salt remains to chap   your lips with aftermath, gone
numb and dry. Still, you will risk   kissing Ken's cheek and leave
your mark. You hear his silence.   He decides to not call it
a scar. You listen hard but   find no malice, only space
between what might become scarred,   should he choose to call it that,
and what neither of you are   ready to dive in, not yet
the swimmer you imagine   each of you might someday be.

FLOODS ARE NOTHING A MIND WILL FULLY GRASP

Floods are nothing a mind will   fully grasp but mind can be
spellbound, as if it were one   of an audience
in an amphitheater,   rapt by a symphony of
virtuoso performers.   The audience will believe
it's the sound, not what's tidal   within sound. What only seems
inaudible, but is its   primary force—most potent
element of music's core   breathing each listener back
to themselves, beyond any   experience of the known,
beyond what "knowing" had meant   to them, to you. You come to
this, as you listen—a friend   cries as she tells you, with her
breath-pauses more than with words,   that she will no longer stare
into her husband's photo   in its frame, no longer will
she believe her memory.   Memories etched in her skin
as the wrinkles that folded   deep and hid how little of
their lives were her choices. She   is crying, folding her face
as if it's paper, she makes   something unexpected—this
folded expression she will   offer you. It is a swan.

THE POEM COULD BE GENEROUS

The poem could be generous   if you'd wash off the candy
surface of use and purpose   you coat around each thing that
would otherwise just float in   and out of what meanings you
make of it, gifting you with   a multiplicity that
advertisements work so hard   to have. You ignore there's a
cloud over the palm trees on   the freeway you take every
night home that is a door. When   you weren't looking it was tagged
with intricate initials   by a graffiti artist
whose words are her real body.   You heard a pulse of it as
a ray of light shining off   a poet reading in a
café last night. Her voice was   echoing all the way back
to the first poem you picked up   as a child. Its rotating
orbit of colors and shapes   an aperture that's open
still.

YOUR MOTHER. IN THE KITCHEN

Your mother. In the kitchen.   Rinsing her hands. Why won't she
turn her eyes to look at you?   How old were you then? You'd asked
something. What was it? Do you   imagine the reason she
doesn't hear you is because   you don't exist? Could this be
memory? Or just better   than to watch her burning eyes
burn right through you. She possessed   that skill. Willpower will scald.
Her gift. Your inheritance.   Claim it. Flaring to surround
you in your own horizon   of fire. What it burns is
of no consequence. You pride   yourself on the way it turns
your hunger to ash. See it   in your eyes after a day
you have eaten so little.   Nothing you'd wanted from her
would have fed you as well as   you feed yourself with this blaze.
Don't type more. Don't ask farther   into the conflagration.
Shut the laptop. Get up. Walk   out your door into your yard.
Into what you are or aren't   seeing in this patch of weeds.
Roses gone wild brown-leaved and   a few soft-lit buds. Inner
lit with a will of their own.   Can it already be spring
again in the compact yard   of this house where you've lived these
twenty years? Must have just rained.   The gravel glints and tinsels.
Reach exhausted hands into   soil still freshly damp. The smell
soothing as a memory   you trust. It's your Nonna's house
a chair gently squeaks floorboards in an upstairs room where she's
rocking your aunt's child toward sleep.   Would it be soothing if you

could unwind the layerings   of memory? Have you will
enough to burn away all   but what you savor? Is it
valiant to use will to say   "forest" when you walk through trees
that are hemmed in on one side   by the highway? Your ears shut
to traffic-noise. Eyes nearly
shut.

NARROW NEGOTIATIONS (6th)

Your husband's face exists where
your exhale ended and your

inhale is premonition
of who you might become if

you see how each breath destroys
what last filled your lungs. Just as

sky is ransacked by first light.
Hidden corridors in its

upper stories creak but show
only clouds when you look up

as you reach out to touch it.
His face is just wind flowing

through the smoke that makes it seem
for an instant visible.

BEFORE YOUR AFFLICTION, WOULD YOU'VE SEEN THE HOBBLING MAN?

Before your affliction, would   you have seen the hobbling man?
Unsteadily he stands, waits.   "Spare change" is just a concept
to you, not a threat-sentence   of life or death. You see him,
now, you think you can relate.   Your back problem will heal, says
the doctor. You are lucky   to have money to pay him.
But the man is thick with scabs   of grime. This morning, one more
button's thread gives up on your   good sweater. The button, you
can't find picks at your worry.   Small loss, like an infection
seethes under surface meanings   of how frayed is the border
between your life and his—no   place tonight for him to sleep.
On the street, all stitching   rots. Your pant leg would open
and drag, your shirt fray. Soon   would nakedness be all you
have left—an all too likely   future that you struggle to
camouflage. The present is   even harder to allow
yourself to see—that you live   on a rim of a dormant
volcano, amassed of what   only appears to be dead
stone. It is actually   ruined bodies. People—with
savings, summer vacations,   with expense accounts—have stacked
the corpses so as to have   the place where they stand. Where you,
too, just barely hold on. Don't   look below you, won't describe
what you see. How simple to   get away with that, until
you can't. The stench not so strong,   yet, to overwhelm you with
recognition, as you spend   so much energy on your
wariness, exhausting your   lumbar-region now, but soon,

all your bones. Still, this stench is   surrounding the man. He is
at the corner you daily   walk past, and though, before your
affliction, you often did   drop change in his hand. Did you
ever look, look so as to   really see him? Will you now?
Or are you afraid one look   will cast you down off the rim?

SIRENS RANSACK THE SPACE IN YOUR MIND

Sirens ransack the space in   your mind, stealing what others
call "memory." But you know   better than to box the night's
stink of the past in a word   no one uses the same way,
that you only recognize   in cliché, a tide sucking
you under what you can't choose,   can only run and never
fast enough in the drifts of   sand. You stumble again, fall.
Not only in your night-sweat.   "You've developed a falling
pattern" the chiropractor   says about your many times
finding yourself on pavement,   on asphalt, on the waxed floor
of the airport. Another   missed plane. Tonight, the siren
stops on your block. Ambulance,   again. Look out your window—
none of the neighbors do you   know. Two houses down, same house
last week. Anonymity   is a sieve, its holes ever
widening. Siren-living   begins with siren breathing.
Too many nights you wake up   short of breath. You see the back
of the ambulance is shut   already, the siren starts.
Someone else is being sucked   into a wave-trough. Will it
let them come up in time to   breathe? Inside your mind someone
is arguing against this,   your neatly contrived construct
that you think has sealed itself   shut. You don't remember your
mother's voice, but it sucks all   the air inside your mind through
the holes of what you want to   call your anonymity. She
left you voiceless. Tonight you   argue back—an argument
you might not want to forget.

CLICHÉS LAST BECAUSE THEY ARE USEFUL

Clichés last because they are   useful. Stories hidden in
repeatable words that come   when the story could be gleaned
to forestall a misstep you're   prone to make, a fall from what
should have been familiar. You've   tumbled in the dark, grabbing
at actual nothingness,   which is what your cells swim in,
though mostly invisible   to the naked eye. But can
cliché see more? "Mist" is a   calming word, mist in your eyes,
it is not that you might be   irreparably blind. You
had been thinking about caged   canaries that the cliché
says miners use—predictive   of invisible peril
of asphyxiation. You   can't hear them in this city—
but can watch for signs of when   they stop. That woman who wears
her Rolex, large and loose and   flashing on her wrist in its
superiority as   she rides BART. You saw her this
morning. Her gaze a tightrope   she believes she's skilled enough
to walk, laughing with friends, as   she heads to a future that she
believes unshakeable, that   she's not balanced on fishing
wire toward a sharp hook. Sirens   outside your window again. It's
4 am. It's an hour   for listening with closed eyes.
Hear the canary in your   sleeplessness? Let yourself tell
your own story from it. How   mist will waft into caverns
of consciousness you hadn't   known surrounded you, where language

is your tightrope, where one word   unexpectedly follows
another to the page, in   which a self you don't know yet
is a wet branch of linden,   still clinging to burnished leaves
for an instant more, before   the inevitable. Your
words can look up, shake the branch,   show you the necessity
of their fall, their signal that   nothing's what it was, even
just a few moments ago.

THE PAUSE IS THIN

The pause is thin. Easily   missed until you fall inside
what is decades long. It waits   beside the thin-tipped felt pen
you reach for to write yourself   until you are only words
you might cross out on a whim.   Keeping notes practical gives
no opportunity for   the pause to extend, enlarge.
No straying itch on your hand   that you can't catch to scratch.
No attitude that something's wrong   if there's no hiatus where
it'll find the fresh straw strewn   by the hand that keeps the cage
locked. No cage. No hand that keeps   the empty bottle of pills.
To remind that you are not,   and will not, do that again.
"You aren't doing that again"   is your latest obsession,
latest attempt to recall   something already grayed-out.
What happens still will happen   regardless of your methods
of control. Insight released   in language may not need
to be tricked to show itself.   Counts are a circus pony
you keep forcing to perform.   You feed it and train it so
the crowd will watch it, not you.   Will you keep obsessively
counting? A collector who   hides in her museum of all
the syllables you hope will   find for you a new meaning
in a line. Of grams on the kitchen scale.   Of times you open every
book on your shelf and read just   the last three words to record
in your notebook, while being   as frightened that they will speak
to you something unknown, or   worse, unknowable as if

you're walking ankle deep in   white dust that rises with each
step, as if you're in a long   ago dried-up ocean bed
and yet waves begin to form.   Turn your eyes away from there
and count to ten. Look again.   You can count this as merely
another irksome "isn't   there" like so many others
that are making a ruckus   in any room where you aren't.

CAN'T FIND ANY WAY TO START

Can't find any way to start.   But why should it matter since
beginnings don't really count.   You can't add them up. They're just
going to fight each other for   ascendancy. The way this
day begins demands that you   see it as being nothing
like the last. Today's the day you will *not*   let the bathroom scale's number
dismay you. Which makes you more   vulnerable. There's so much
cruelty in everyone's   eyes to whom you must tell "no"
as a matter of ethics   and professionalism.
How can the scale's increase make   you naked to corrosive
rain that angry people can   force down from the sky? Yet this
day's other way to begin   battles for supremacy.
If you see you're not the same   weight as yesterday then you
will simply eat less. It won't   be that much less. No worry
that this is exactly what   you did yesterday and you'll
not worry how many days   like this you've lived.
You pride yourself that you are   no longer the girl hiding
in your bathroom to vomit.   You're no longer the woman
who has a boyfriend smoking   in the garage arguing
with his prison-tattooed friends.   You have the insight to hear
how hypnotic is the hum   of your channel-surfing. But
rising from its stupor asks   more. Acknowledge one place to
seek safety and you begin   to see others. Even now
will you reach for the easy   metaphor of a seed deep
in soil cracking open to   free a green shoot reaching up
toward light, toward life? Will you keep   writing only what you know?
You have hidden there too long.   Self-starving as protection

isn't only about food.　　Somewhere on your shelf there's still
Bolaño's book of stories　　you closed before asking what
was in the quote you couldn't　　understand. Or didn't you
want to savor what frightened　　in his *huddled breathing shape?*
Didn't want a taste in its　　meaning you couldn't turn from?
Couldn't deny? Can you want　　　to cup it in your hands? To
listen and tell its story　　　with your own pen and ink? Could
a story you begin find　　an ending this time? Rather
than adding wrinkles to what　　　you call your hands. Look down.
Are
they really hands? Or do you　　　just have two arms that end in
violence equipped with an　　accessible inviting
style?

THERE'S THAT MAN AGAIN

There's that man again. He's back   on the street corner. Eyes closed
he reaches with both arms and   seems to catch the thing he wants
deftly cupping it in his hands.   He doesn't have to look at

you to know you can't see it.   You've your own reaching to do,
which you mostly keep to your   self, curtained-off or quelled. But
today you want to ask, "Is   there, by chance, a bearable

speed in which time will settle   so you won't miss what happens?"
You fall into step with a   woman walking ahead of
you. Your body matching her   movements. Who you are expands

because of this encounter.   Could your fate somehow have been
altered? Impossible to   know. Do not overtake her.
It's not her face that matters.   Just what you don't really grasp

that you pass to someone else.   Learning how to die may come
as a posture adapted   from glimpses of circumstance.
Once you saw a pigeon dead   on the street and couldn't stop

staring until staring did
not need to make the pigeon
move.

NARROW NEGOTIATIONS (7th)

You lie under the covers.
The window wide for any

breeze. Better than sleep to be
deep in night's tall grass. Silence

isn't ruined but advanced
by frog's guttural echo

of your forgotten desire
to be an animal made

permeable by the sounds
outside what ears apprehend.

The noise when sentience rips
through night's starless cover that

shifts what day will be. Frog hears
and comes investigating.

TO THE RAG YOU HAVE BEEN, SPEAK DIRECTLY

To the rag you have been, speak directly. You've rubbed with it
down to recognitions you'll hide from no longer. When young
you would scrub the silence a man gives until you were
thread-bare, until you couldn't pretend anymore to clean
and polish his brass badges worn for the violations
he performed, whatever the narrative he wanted
believed by the other men, who, like him, police the street
as if entitled to make their order the controlling
force. You remember soaking in the tub. He's with his friends
in a bar prophesying from the bottom of the next
tequila bottle, a new empire he'll construct, just as soon
as they find one more victim who will front them one more round.
You turn on the tap. Water— so hot it's absolution—
draws from you a kind of voice existing before language
came linearly from mind to tongue as a progression.
Utterance that calls back to what began in uterus—
clarvoyancies across time yet simple as steam comes to
coalesce around you, comes as kin to transformation.
The rag answers wordlessly. It knows the pride that first
begins in defiance, that begins as you cast off your
wanting him back home. Wring out, from the rag you are, what is
born of abjection, birthed as the violent flapping of wings.
Red-eyed carrion seeker who'll find, in you, your own meal.
You begin by consuming the deaths you carry within.

TO THE RAG, SAY SUFFERING WASN'T YOUR PURPOSE

To the rag, say suffering   wasn't your purpose. On your
knees, you heard linoleum   speak to the rag in your hand,
the rag gripped in your knuckles,   the grimy rivulets of
decades would break free. Future   started as thickness you rubbed
hard, some futures could ruin   the hands. But the muscles you
built surprised—you could trust them.   Rag began as confidant—
had been a blouse you'd worn down   to threadbare, soft. No one bought
you another. You didn't   need one, didn't go out where
a blouse is a requirement   for the risky commerce of
contact. Safe in the house, stitched   together wrath stolen from
Mother's closet. A dark blue   fabric to most eyes, to yours,
a color to fall inside,   who knows if each time you could
find your way back. Mother was   bulimic, Father, a tall
glass of bourbon at each meal,   then, as his meal, he consumed
himself. Neither of them could   care what grew wild, filled the floor—
tangled ivy, thorn bushes   you were small enough to slide
between to find coins, sometimes   dollars, some 10s, and even
once a 20. A rag was   camouflage. As if always
scrubbing, knowing the wild would   one day fill the house, and you'd
need to get out. Thought it'd   be easy, never come back.
You'd just stand up, but a rag   is what you'd become. All these
dollars and how could a rag   spend them, where you weren't welcome.

Now, decades later, decades   that are only an instant
of the endlessness within   each sensation the rag holds—
a full moon still visible   in your pale morning intake
of breath, five red-winged black birds   rising in all directions,
your eyes, you realize, can   follow each one of them.

A CATERPILLAR

A caterpillar on this   beach where you're walking miles from
shrubs. How did it crawl so far?   Last night's storm left a leafless
branch on your porch. Its many   twig-ends pointing at nothing

you can follow. Though you can't   stop listening at every
deep recess of its quiet.   Some silences just stay wide.
You watched for a long time your   mom's mouth fallen open at

death. A shape that your mouth can't   mimic. Some silence thickens
to a mask that you can't stop   wearing. Abrasive as sand
granules you try to rub from   your skin as if they weren't skin

and beneath them you'd find what's
real as the earth waiting for
you.

WROTE A QUOTE IN YOUR NOTEBOOK

Wrote a quote in your notebook.   But not where you found we love
to hold the continual   failure in one another.
Some books open like people.   You feel their eyes on you and
the prickle up your spine but   a chance of any deeper

recognition turns you from   them instead of toward. Easy
to wish now that you'd kept some   reference point when you no
longer recall what the risk   was. Though doesn't it tickle
your flesh just to consider?   Like an insect you are sure

is there and you scratch the spot   ˙ hard before you see you've left
a mark? Reading can be like   having the kind of sex that
makes your body into a   country where they tell you that
every vote counts. Even if   one and one and one vote just

doesn't add up. Won't save you   when the phone starts ringing and
it's your surgery calling.   Didn't pay the bill. Didn't
open the demand notice.
Blame yourself for the hiding   you've done. Don't even try to

remember when it started   since memory is what you
first learned to hide from. Then came   the guilt of having done that
to yourself. Even to type   this and keep your attention
with the thought you intend means   scratching at an insect still

biting just below the skin   which is premonition's skin.
You'd be willing to make it   bleed if that might be how you'd
feel something like the friction   between sky and branch when wind
is still invisible to   anything but the tree's bark.

Already minutely it   has begun cracking in what
will be a hurricane force.   Isn't this something that
you maybe had written down   before but so quickly chose
to forget. Will you again?   *The language of all others   is unintelligible*

retorts Bolaño in a   used copy of ANTWERP you
hadn't realized you were   looking for. It's a quote you'd
underlined. What you had thought   he meant already changing
as you read from one word to   the next. The language that is

your own might just be the most   unintelligible of
all and the "others" inside   you are some of the others
he saw but left just below   the page's skin for you to
scratch down to find. Don't worry   why this was the random page

you happened to open to.   Turn more pages, and see in
the very sentence that you   begin to read, another
quote with its eyes open, and   this time you look back. It's not
intelligibility   that the quote offers, nor what

you want to see visible,   but the *traces of recent
fires.*

NARROW NEGOTIATIONS (8th)

A burial-ground drumbeat
you dreamt. A risk to recall.

To hear how its rhythms are
receptors. Birds use their own

to make holes in the sky when
ever they need to vanish.

How much better to live each
instant as if already

behind you. That's how gnats spin
holes in air and then slip through.

Until ground sucked you under,
your hands didn't know digging

isn't about escape, but
finding worms, moles, your lost limbs.

Notes

Syllable-counting constraints

In writing these poems, I initially was convinced that a limitation in the form could speak to me about how much I let myself perceive the limitations I inflict upon myself, versus those that are unavoidable in my life. By using a constraining form, I would not just write *about limitation*, I'd live inside limitation in the work and then see how I handled it. I would experience limitation as event, not aftermath.

Ann Lauterbach points out that the "convergence of subject matter with form releases content." The form I created can cause a contentiousness in my use of syntax that forces me to diverge from my more expected trajectories of thought, and so it exposes a content with more contextual resources than I'd had access to.

But contrived structures can obscure as much as they reveal; my obsessions are powerful. I had to let the poems continue to ask me if I was writing in support of my intuitions about freedom or sometimes avoiding them. Once I saw, in the writing, how easily I can delude myself, I started to see it in my life.

Hélène Cixous tells us "the border makes up the homeland, it prohibits and gives passage in the same stroke." My work is to see where the borders, the framings, I use to contain my understanding are useful, and where they are borders that I must open and pass beyond, frightening as that might be.

Besides these poems, there are also poems scattered throughout the manuscript that are all titled "Narrow Negotiations." In these, the form is this: each has exactly seven couplets (14 lines per poem). Each line in the poem has seven syllables (as does the title "Narrow Negotiations").

Quotes in these poems

In some of the poems, I've incorporated quotes (in italics, and at times in quotation marks) from authors whose work has been provocation and inspiration to me. The authors of those quotes are named in the poems.

At times, I use quotation marks to emphasize a word that I'm attempting to draw special attention to.

Grateful acknowledgment

to the following journals where these poems were originally published
(some in earlier versions):

Boston Review (*2 poems*: "you rub"; "hear news anchors)"

Lana Turner (*3 poems*: walked out; light flickers; no wild)

Lit Hub (*3 poems*: bleach trees; you lie in the yard; you envy cyclists)

The Iowa Review (*2 poems*: can't find any way; wrote the quote)

The Colorado Review (*3 poems*: tragedy has; learned to stay; a state of)

Fence (*2 poems*: hear wind cipher; your latest cure for landscape)

The Academy of American Poets *Poem-a-Day* (*2 poems*: crowded; in the flood)

rob meclennan's curated selections on MEDIUM (*2 poems*: you buy disposable; reach)

Oversound (*2 poems*: sleeplessness; you don't)

River Styx (*2 poems*: you've put your unease; it's first daylight)

Prelude (*2 poems*: who are you living for; even when not engaged)

The Obscure Lives of Poets (anthology) (*1 poem*: the poem could be generous)

USA Jubilee Edition of Enchanting Verses Literary Review (*1 poem*: a caterpillar)

Bosque (*1 poem*: through your open window)

New Limestone Review (*2 poems*: curve of; your husband's)

Spillway (*1 poem*: there's that man again standing)

Ocean (*1 poems*: come on then)

The February Project (*1 poem*: hand-out dollar ready)

White Stag (*1 poem*: actual listening)

Touch the Donkey (*1 poem*: thought there'd still be)